BABY SIGN LANGUAGE

D1226232

STERLING INNOVATION
New York

An Imprint of Sterling Publishing
387 Park Avenue South
New York, NY 10016

STERLING INNOVATION and the distinctive Sterling Innovation logo
are registered trademarks of Sterling Publishing Co., Inc.

Designed by Tim Palin Creative

Illustrations by Dan Crisp

The publisher would like to thank all of the parents who graciously allowed their children's
stories and photos to be used. The publisher also would like to acknowledge the following
for permission to reproduce their royalty-free photographs: Rubberball Productions:
Cover, 6, 9, 12, 18, 22, 26, 32, 37, 40, 62, 64, 74, 79, 88, 98; Corbis: 28, 85;
Photodisc (Getty Images): 43, 48, 71, 83, 102; Ablestock: 67;
Hi-Tech Photo: 120; Thinkstock: 5, 25, 116

ISBN 978-1-4351-5251-9

This book is part of the Baby Sign Language kit and is not to be sold separately.

For information about custom editions, special sales, and premium and corporate
purchases, please contact Sterling Special Sales at 800-805-5489 or
specialsales@sterlingpublishing.com.

Manufactured in China

2 4 6 8 10 9 7 5 3 1

www.sterlingpublishing.com

BABY SIGN LANGUAGE

FIND OUT WHAT'S ON YOUR BABY'S MIND!

Karine Shemel Rosenberg

STERLING INNOVATION
New York

CONTENTS

CHAPTER 1: Welcome to Baby Sign Language. . . 6

CHAPTER 2: Baby Sign Language Basics. 22

CHAPTER 3: Starter Words 48

CHAPTER 4: Reinforcing Baby Sign Language . . 64

CHAPTER 5: Advanced Baby Signs 74

CHAPTER 6: Fun with Baby Sign Language. 88

Dictionary of Baby Signs 102

Index 117

About the Author 120

CHAPTER ONE

Welcome to Baby Sign Language

WHY DO PARENTS TURN TO BABY SIGN LANGUAGE?

All parents keep their ears open for the magical day when their child utters his or her first recognizable word. In the meantime, infants rely on smiling, cooing, and crying to communicate. Gestures and nonverbal sounds function as a baby's language before he or she is ready for the spoken word. These facial expressions, body movements, and sounds are precursors of baby sign language.

There are hundreds of "baby sign language" signals that can be learned by both babies and their parents in order to facilitate preverbal communication. Some of these signs are universal, while others will be unique to parent and child.

Baby sign language is excellent practice for parents seeking ways to bond with their babies as well as ease their frustration. It is a perfect introduction to the lifelong communication that occurs between parent and child.

WHAT ARE BABY SIGNS?

Baby signs are simple, easy-to-use-and-remember gestures used by parents and their babies to communicate better with each other. Babies are able to "talk" about things they see and feel but for which they don't yet have words. The use of gestures will also enhance future verbal interactions between you and your baby. Possibly the greatest aspect of baby sign language is that it is easy to learn and use. You do not have to enroll in a course or be certified in American Sign Language (ASL). All it takes is using gestures to enhance specific words. With time, your baby will learn the same gestures you have modeled. Congratulations! Your baby is signing!

Horse

> *"* There is no greater gift that you can give your child at the beginning of life than the ability to communicate. *"*

*Dr. Sally Ward,
Babytalk*

Your child is probably already using signs without you even realizing it!

HOW IS BABY SIGN LANGUAGE DIFFERENT FROM ASL?

American Sign Language (commonly referred to as ASL) is a visual-gestural language used as a primary means of communication between many hearing-challenged people. In ASL, facial expressions, such as raising or lowering of eyebrows and body language, are integral parts of communication. These actions help give meaning to what is being signed, much like vocal tones and inflections give meaning to spoken words.

Some parents who sign with their hearing babies prefer to limit themselves to ASL signs. Still, many parents who have attempted baby sign language find it to be just as—and sometimes even more—rewarding of a language. The most important thing to remember when choosing one type of signing language to work with is that babies do not actually use the signs as a true "language." That will come later.

The main goal in using baby sign language is to facilitate communication between parent and child. Baby sign language incorporates signs from ASL and combines them with signs created by babies and their parents.

// In a nutshell, the signing babies outperformed the other babies in comparison after comparison. They scored higher in intelligence tests, understood more words, had larger vocabularies, and engaged in more sophisticated play. //

Linda Acredolo and Susan Goodwyn, Baby Signs

WHEN AND WHERE DID BABY SIGN LANGUAGE ORIGINATE?

In the late 1980s, Linda Acredolo and Susan Goodwyn, professors at the University of California, Davis, studied the impact of baby sign language on preverbal children. Funded by a grant from the National Institute of Child Health and Human Development, their study showed that children who signed outperformed non-signing children in many areas of cognitive and language development.

In another study, Dr. Joseph Garcia of the University of Alaska was intrigued by his observations that babies of deaf parents became sign-language "experts" by the age of nine months. Garcia also noted that babies of hearing parents did not communicate nearly as much at nine months of age. His study, like the one conducted by Acredolo and Goodwyn, concentrated on the implications of baby sign language on a child's cognitive and language development.

WHAT ARE SOME RECENT DEVELOPMENTS IN THE FIELD?

Over the past 20 years, additional research has been conducted that shows the benefits of signing for preverbal children. In the mid-1990s, studies proved that the practice of signing with a child in no way deters or delays that child from later speaking. In fact, results showed that learning to sign actually encourages early spoken communication in babies.

Based on these significant research studies and sign language programs, many grassroots baby sign language programs have emerged. Most of today's programs are based on ASL and share the same goal: to facilitate a preverbal child's cognitive and verbal development.

Sleep

"The child is a veritable image of becoming, of possibility, poised to reach towards what is not yet, towards a growing that cannot be predetermined or prescribed. I see her and I fill the space with others like her, risking, straining, wanting to find out, to ask their own questions, to experience a world that is shared."

Maxine Greene, U.S. philosopher and educator

TOP 5 REASONS WHY PARENTS LOVE BABY SIGN LANGUAGE

1. BABY SIGNS WILL HELP YOUR BABY TALK SOONER.

Ball

Many parents wonder what sort of effect sign language will have on their child's speech development, but numerous studies show that babies who sign will talk sooner than non-signers. Signing babies also use "expressive language" or "verbal language," combining words and ideas long before they are able to speak.

2. BABY SIGNS WILL EMPOWER YOUR BABY TO INITIATE CONVERSATION.

Think about how often your baby has shown signs that he or she wants to communicate. Your baby may raise his arms to tell you "Pick me up!" or reach for things that he wants. Your baby may open her mouth to show you that she is hungry. Baby sign language expands on this initiative by allowing your child to communicate about specific ideas and concepts, like which toy he wants to play with or which type of juice she wants to drink. Once your child shows an interest in a specific topic, you will be able to elaborate on that interest by modeling the appropriate language with the accompanying gesture.

Juice

3. BABY SIGNS WILL REDUCE YOUR CHILD'S FRUSTRATION.

Parents and researchers agree that babies who sign have fewer moments of frustration. Many parents remark that once they start signing, the frequency of their child's tantrums diminish. Signing also enables parents to redirect and discipline their children in public without the use of loud voices—thus avoiding embarrassing moments! Finally, baby sign gestures can and will replace a child's whining and grunting with clear expressions of thought.

My tooth hurts!

My diaper needs changing!

I'm hungry!

One of the main causes of a baby's tears is his or her frustration at not being understood.

4. BABY SIGNS BUILD A FOUNDATION FOR EARLY LITERACY SKILLS.

Children love books. Baby signs can make those books even more meaningful to your child. Your baby can be an active participant during story time, such as labeling pictures or predicting the next action. This type of active participation will help your baby understand the concepts targeted by the author.

Book

5. BABY SIGNS WILL STIMULATE YOUR CHILD'S INTELLECTUAL DEVELOPMENT.

Research has shown that adding sign language to verbal communication will enhance a preschool child's vocabulary, spelling, and early reading skills. Marilyn Daniels, researcher and author of *Dancing with Words: Signing for Hearing Children's Literacy*, discovered that hearing students in pre-kindergarten who were able to use sign language elements in both verbal and written language scored significantly higher on standardized vocabulary tests than those hearing students with no sign language instruction.

Music/Song

NOAH SIGNS AT THE DOCTOR'S OFFICE

Two-year-old Noah was up all night with a cough that didn't seem to want to go away. The next morning, Noah was uncharacteristically quiet and ate very little breakfast. Eli, his dad, decided it was time to see the pediatrician.

When the doctor took out her stethoscope, Noah signed *hurt* by touching his index fingers together and up to his throat, indicating his throat hurt. Eli translated Noah's message, and the doctor responded to Noah, saying, "Now I know that your throat hurts. Let me take a look at it so we can help you feel better."

In the end, despite his sore throat, Noah was able to communicate to the doctor using sign language.

CHAPTER TWO
Baby Sign Language Basics

HOW DO I START SIGNING WITH MY BABY?

Getting started is easy! Sit on the floor or bend down so that you are in your baby's direct line of vision. Once you have your child's full attention, you can begin to sign a word. Say the spoken word at the same time you sign so your baby understands what the gesture means. Baby sign language is about making the connection between spoken word and gesture.

As you begin signing, keep the words in context to what you are doing. For example, if you are teaching your baby the sign for *cereal*, introduce and show her the sign during breakfast. Signs should be motivating and exciting for your child, so pick words that your child will want to learn. If your child loves dolls, teach the sign for *baby* or *bottle* during playtime. Make signing time as natural as you can and include signing in your day-to-day routines. Remember, the more consistent you are with signing, the quicker your baby will learn it!

HINTS ON HOW TO SUCCESSFULLY SIGN WITH YOUR CHILD

- Get your baby's attention before you begin signing.

- Have your baby see the object and your sign at the same time.

- A spoken word should always accompany the gesture.

- Start by using simple words such as *milk*, *more*, and *all gone*.

- Keep family members and other caregivers in the loop about your child's progress.

- Demonstrate to others the signs your baby is likely to use.

- Be creative and make up your own special signs.

- Follow your child's lead and model signs that he or she wants to learn about.

- Praise your child's attempts consistently.

- Give your child time. It may take your child several months to produce a first sign.

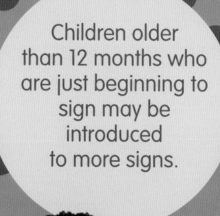

Children older
than 12 months who
are just beginning to
sign may be
introduced
to more signs.

HOW DO I CHOOSE THE FIRST SIGNS?

When choosing first signs, consider ones that will be easy for your baby to do as well as those that represent useful concepts. Choose three to five signs that represent things that your child sees or does repeatedly from daily routines and/or are highly motivating (animals, toys, pets). Some starter signs from a child's routine may include *eat*, *drink*, *more*, and *milk*. Starter signs that are highly motivating may include *cat*, *dog*, *book*, and *flower*.

Focus on these signs for a few weeks before adding new ones. Don't overload your baby! Stick with the first signs you have introduced until he or she can start making them.

Once you feel your baby has caught on to the concept of baby signs, he or she is ready for more. Gradually add more signs, while continuing to use the starter signs.

" When we are curious about a child's words and our responses to those words, the child feels respected. The child is respected. *"*

Vivian Paley

Infants are born with an innate desire for attention, contact, and interaction.

28

HOW DO I CHOOSE
THE FIRST SIGNS?

Although there is no specific age, researchers recommend that the optimal time to start signing with your child falls somewhere between six to eight months of age. This is when babies first develop an interest in the process. Researchers caution against introducing baby sign language before this time because babies under six months of age have little long-term memory and are unable to retain signs. They also lack the motor skills and hand-eye coordination required to make gestures. It is important for you, as a parent, to watch your baby's interest in communication and make that the focus, as opposed to the actual age of your baby.

Whatever your baby's age, before your baby is ready to sign, he or she must be able to understand what *you* are signing. This understanding will be the first step towards a two-way conversation.

Eventually, your baby will repeat a sign back to you—your baby's first sign! Initially, the sign will most probably be one that you have modeled. It may take some time before your baby begins to spontaneously sign to you. Remember, for your child to begin signing, he or she needs to be able to think of something and then remember the appropriate sign.

Between six to eight months of age is the optimum time to introduce signing.

Hi/Bye

You have probably already introduced your baby to signs without realizing it. Waving hello and bye-bye, pointing, blowing kisses, shaking and nodding your head are common signs that babies and toddlers pick up quickly. Using more signs to communicate with your child will be just as simple!

Remember, every baby's agenda is different and is based on his or her interests, rate of development, and experiences.

Before you know it, your newborn will be ready to sign.

SIGNS THAT YOUR BABY MAY BE READY FOR BABY SIGN LANGUAGE:

- Your baby points to things.

- Your baby waves bye-bye.

- Your baby shakes his or her head "yes" and "no."

- Your baby looks for a response when showing you an item.

- Your baby is interested in picture books.

- Your baby is frustrated when you do not understand his or her wants and needs.

IS IT EVER TOO LATE TO TEACH BABY SIGN LANGUAGE?

No. Even if your baby has already begun saying a few words, you can still teach baby sign language. Signing enhances language development, so you will probably notice your baby picking up new vocabulary words faster. Therefore, it's a good idea to introduce words that your baby does not yet have. Continue to use the same modeling techniques with more difficult words. If your child is already speaking, you will find that pairing up the sign with an already existing word will produce the best results. For example, if your child already has the word *eat* in her spoken vocabulary, you can model the sign for *cereal*. At breakfast, your baby may then gesture *cereal* while saying *eat*.

Even after toddlers are able to say the word, their pronunciation is not always clear. Hand gestures, or signs, are easier to interpret, especially when they are combined with a garbled spoken word.

- Use speech that is clear and simple for your child to model.

- Repeat what your child has signed.

- Ask your child questions, beginning with yes/no questions.

- Expand your child's vocabulary. Start by naming body parts. Build and expand on what your child says.

- Sing songs and nursery rhymes.

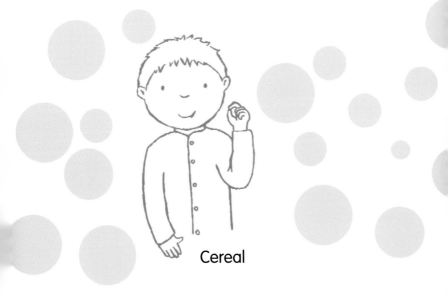

Cereal

WHAT IS A TYPICAL BABY'S RATE OF LANGUAGE DEVELOPMENT?

All babies develop at their own rate. The same way babies learn to speak and use words when they are ready, they will learn to use baby sign language when they are ready! That said, the following is a list of language milestones you may notice in your baby. Between the ages of six and nine months, most babies will begin to:

- comprehend simple words.

- look at family members when their names are called.

- babble with singsong patterns.

- understand and react to facial expressions.

- attempt gestures.

- use more and different types of sounds when babbling.

HOW MANY SIGNS WILL MY BABY LEARN AT FIRST?

Your baby will probably start communicating by using one or two signs to symbolize many things. It is important during this time to be patient and to try and figure out what your baby is trying to sign. Encourage your baby by modeling the sign back to him or her, by talking, and then by using the more appropriate sign that represents the word you believe he or she was trying to communicate.

When your baby catches on to signing, carry your baby sign cards with you everywhere you go!

Soon your baby will begin to understand that there are signs and words for everything! Signing with your baby will become incredibly fun at this point. Suddenly, he or she will want to know everything, and you will realize how much your baby wants to learn as well as how interested your baby is in sharing his or her world with you.

Pig

Monkey

"The limits of my language mean the limits of my world. "

Vivian Paley

WILL SIGNING INTERFERE WITH MY BABY'S SPEECH DEVELOPMENT?

No. In fact, the opposite is usually true. Signing may improve your child's language and vocabulary. As previous researchers have pointed out, signing enhances language; it doesn't replace it. Use signing alongside normal speech so that your baby can make the connection between the gesture and the word.

In time, your baby will say the word he or she is signing because *you* are saying the word each time you sign. As your child's spoken vocabulary grows, you can stop signing those words. However, you may still want to add signs for *new* words.

Remember that although your child may be pronouncing certain words while signing, sometimes only one consonant may be clear. This is why modeling the sign is still useful—it will help you figure out what your child is trying to say!

WHAT WILL THE TRANSITION FROM BABY SIGNS TO SPOKEN LANGUAGE BE LIKE?

Your child's first learned sign will often be the last one he or she stops using. Some children may hold on to signs, even though they are able to vocalize almost everything. If this holding-on pattern continues, encourage your baby to use words. You can do this by dropping all signs and using spoken words only. You can also draw attention to your lips by bringing your finger to your mouth when talking.

Do not pressure your child to stop signing! Gently ease him or her through this transition period. Your baby will begin to let go of each sign as easily as when he or she first learned it!

" A child reminds us that playtime is an essential part of our daily routine. *"*

Anonymous

TOP 10 BABY SIGN LANGUAGE TIPS

Keep these points in mind when signing with your child:

- Be patient. It may take a few months for your infant to produce a first sign.

- Get your child's attention before signing. Use phrases such as, "Come here; I want to show you something."

- Start by using simple words such as *more* and *milk*.

- Pair each spoken word with its sign.

- Follow your child's lead.

- Praise your child's first attempts.

- Be creative and have fun. Make up your own special signs together.

- Include signing during daily routines and playtime.

- Use signs that are important to your child and will motivate him or her.

- Share your child's signs with family members and other caregivers.

Milk

SAMSON'S FIRST SIGN

Jordana and Andy began baby sign language classes with their son Samson when he was nine months old. They had no expectations. They just wanted to have a good time with their son and hoped that he would pick up a few signs along the way. Samson enjoyed the classes, especially all the new toys that were introduced. However, Jordana felt unsure that he was getting anything out of the class. It had been six weeks, and Samson had not yet signed a single word. Jordana wondered if she was modeling the signs correctly or if Samson was just not ready.

Then one day, Jordana sang a song which Samson always enjoyed. The song contains different animal sounds including the meow of a cat. Jordana modeled *cat* by tracing whiskers on her cheek, as she had done several times before. When she reached the second verse, Jordana noticed that Samson was attempting to sign *cat* to her by tracing whiskers on his cheek! She also realized that he was using the sign for all the animal sounds. Jordana was proud that of all the signs that she had begun to use with Samson, *cat* was his first sign!

CHAPTER THREE
Starter Words

WHAT ARE SOME RECOMMENDED STARTER WORDS?

The signs/words on the following pages have been organized into categories based on words that your baby will want to "say" or sign as he or she experiences the world. The deck of cards that come packaged with this book will also be a helpful resource.

❝ One seeks to equip the child with deeper, more gripping, and subtler ways of knowing the world and himself. ❞

Jerome S. Bruner,
U.S. psychologist and educator

MEALTIME SIGNS

Thanks to baby sign language, your child can indicate the foods and drink he or she wants without becoming frustrated. The following mealtime signs will take guessing out of the picture!

Milk
Open and close fists as if milking a cow.

Juice
Place one fist on top of the other fist and twist.

Cookie
Twist fingertips in palm, like a cookie cutter.

Banana
Make a peeling motion down the index finger.

All Gone
Swoop hands from the center outward.

More
Tap fingertips together.

Water
Use extended index, middle, and ring fingers to form a "W." Tap the "W" on the chin twice.

Cereal
Form an "O" with thumb and index finger.

Drink
Tip an imaginary glass to open lips, as if drinking.

Eat
Place fingertips to the lips.

BEDTIME SIGNS

Routines are comforting for children. A bedtime routine helps your baby learn which activities come before others, such as brushing teeth before reading a book. Most babies tend to master the bedtime routine quickly.

Bath
Make fists and rub up and down chest.

Blanket
Grasp and pull up an imaginary blanket with downturned hands.

Pacifier
Suck on thumb and index finger.

Book
Hold hands together and open and close palms.

Quiet
Place index finger across lips.

Sleep
Rest head on hands and tilt head to the side.

Hi/Bye
Hold hand in front of shoulder and wave fingers up and down.

Moon
Raise palm and make circles.

Light
Open and close fists.

Toothbrush
Move finger across teeth.

FEELING SIGNS

By using baby signs, your child can tell you when he or she feels happy, distressed, tired, or hungry!

Afraid
Protect body with palms open while cringing.

Angry
Open and close clawed hand while scowling.

Sad
Trace imaginary tears down cheek.

Happy
With flat hand, pat chest with an upward stroking movement.

Love
*Cross fists
over chest.*

Sorry
*Make a
circle on chest
with fist.*

Share
*Brush the little finger of
one hand back and forth
along the index finger of
other hand as if dividing
something.*

Want
*Hold palms facing
upward and form
claws with fingers,
pulling them
towards body.*

Please
*Place hand
over heart and
move it
in circles.*

**Thank You/
You're
Welcome**
*Pull the fingertips
of one hand away
from chin.*

SAFETY SIGNS

Safety is a major concern for parents raising toddlers. The following signs are useful in helping children avoid accidents and keeping them safe, healthy, and happy.

Hot
With palm out, move hand up and down.

Help
With fist on palm, move palm upward.

Stop
Use side of hand to hit palm sharply.

Wait
With upturned hands, wiggle fingers with the left hand forward.

Cold
Hold arms close to body and shiver.

Hurt
Touch index fingers together.

Gentle
Stroke the back of the opposite hand.

Yes
Make a fist and move it up and down at the wrist while nodding head.

No
Close first two fingers on thumb.

Dirty
Wiggle fingers of right hand under chin.

AT HOME SIGNS

Your baby spends a lot of time at home and is always learning more about the environment around him or herself.

Ball
Trace a ball shape with hands.

Shoe
With thumbs facing inward, hit fists together twice.

Telephone
Hold pinky finger and thumb out and place next to ear.

Music/Song
Move hand back and forth rhythmically.

Play
With thumb and little finger up, twist both hands.

Diaper
Pat hip.

Baby
Make rock-a-bye motion.

Big
Keeping both index fingers and thumbs up, move hands apart.

Little
Face palms together and close.

Hair
Rub hair between fingers.

OUTSIDE SIGNS

The world outside is an exciting place for young children, one where they experience exciting things to see, smell, and hear!

Rain
Wiggle fingers while moving downwards.

Sun
Curve both hands over head.

Car
Make a steering motion with fists.

Airplane
With index and little finger up, swoop hand upward.

Out/Outside
Pull one hand out of the other hand.

Flower
Touch each side of nose with fingers.

Bird
Hold index finger and thumb close to mouth and open and close like a bird's beak.

Dog
Brush the back of one ear a couple of times.

Stars
Raise hands and wiggle fingers.

Train
Move fist up and down as if pulling a whistle.

WHAT WILL THE TRANSITION FROM BABY SIGNS TO SPOKEN LANGUAGE BE LIKE?

Once you have mastered most of the starter words, answer the following questions about your baby's favorite things to determine what additional signs to use. For instance, if your child's favorite song is the "Eensy Weensy Spider," your baby might like to learn how to sign *spider*.

WHAT IS YOUR BABY'S FAVORITE:

pet

play toy

snack

meal

drink

animal

song

book

LILY SIGNS FOR WATER

Two-year-old Lily had been signing for about eight months. Although she primarily used verbal language skills to communicate, Lily continued to sign to her parents when she wanted to emphasize certain words and ideas or when she felt strongly about something.

During lunchtime one afternoon, Lily accidentally spilled her glass of water on the floor. Her mother Victory was busy cooking and speaking on the telephone, with her back turned to Lily. Amidst all the distractions, Victory didn't hear Lily when she asked for water.

When her mother still hadn't responded after several verbal requests for more water, Lily got off her chair, climbed onto the chair next to where her mother was cooking, tugged on her mother's shirt, and signed *water* by forming a "W" with her fingers and tapping the side of her mouth. Lily remembered the sign for *water* and figured out how to use it to get the results she wanted.

CHAPTER FOUR
Reinforcing Baby Sign Language

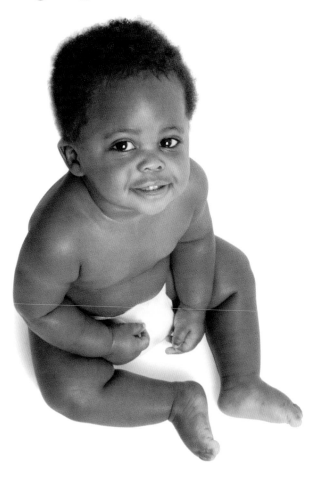

HOW CAN I USE POSITIVE REINFORCEMENT WHEN SIGNING WITH MY BABY?

It is important to positively reinforce your child's signing efforts. Reward your child whenever possible as he or she begins to sign. This will communicate that you understand what he or she is doing and that you are paying attention. For example, if your baby signs *eat*, give him or her some apple slices or crackers, even if it is not yet snack time.

❚❚ A mother understands what a child does not say. **❚❚**

Jewish proverb

WHY SHOULD I INVOLVE OTHERS IN THE BABY SIGN LANGUAGE PROCESS?

For working parents, making the decision to sign with your baby may be a difficult one. Working parents may feel they don't have enough consistency between home and/or daycare to start a program with their children. Parents who work may also be uncertain as to whether or not their child's daycare will support their baby sign language process.

Once a parent has decided to use baby signs with a child, it is important to involve everyone who cares for and interacts with that child on a regular basis. Your baby's signing progress will improve much more quickly if you can get other family members, caregivers, and friends on board.

> **"** Whoever influences the child's life
> ought to try to give him a positive
> view of himself and of his world. **"**

Bruno Bettelheim, A Good Enough Parent

With positive reinforcement, your child will realize the power of signing and attempt to sign more often.

HOW CAN I MAKE IT EASIER FOR OTHERS TO SUPPORT MY BABY'S SIGNING DEVELOPMENT?

Start by explaining your child's signing program in detail. You might even refer them to a specific video or book with signs that can be easily referenced. Another option is to copy and post picture cards in relevant areas. Hang cards with bath time signs in the bathroom or cards with mealtime signs near the highchair.

Banana

Keep the consistency between home and daycare by:

- letting your caregiver know from the beginning that you are signing with your baby.

- demonstrating the signs your baby is most likely to use.

- providing caretakers with a sign language book as reference.

- letting your child's caregiver know which signs you are working on.

- giving permission to your child's caregivers to introduce new signs, too.

Toothbrush

WHAT ARE MADE-UP SIGNS?

Made-up signs are commonly referred to as "home signs." Parents are encouraged to create their own signs with their child and should strive for signs that will also be easily understood by other family members and caregivers.

Many babies will experiment with creating their own signs. Parents should watch for any unusual actions that their babies seem to be doing repeatedly and with determination. These will likely be simple actions that are related to the objects around them. Many times, your baby will be looking at you, trying to determine if you understand what he or she is gesturing.

If your baby makes up a sign, you can decide to keep it and use it or you can respond to your child by saying the word and using the ASL version of the sign. If you use the ASL version repeatedly, your child will eventually follow your lead and sign that version. As a general rule, it is always best to use ASL signs for routine items and actions and for those things that are important to your child.

MADE-UP BABY SIGNS SHOULD:

- resemble the objects they represent.

- use big movements and be simple for a baby to make.

- be clearly different from other signs your baby knows.

ERIN'S LIGHT SHOW

Keith and Deirdre never dreamed of using baby sign language with their daughter. However, when Erin turned nine months old, they discovered that signing was the easiest way to communicate with her. Neither parent was familiar with American Sign Language, so they created their own "home signs" with their daughter.

Certain signs were especially helpful to Keith and Deidre when it came to understanding what Erin wanted. When Erin was thirteen months old, they took her to have professional pictures taken at a photography studio. Typical of most toddlers, Erin was uncooperative, deciding that she was going to play with the toys around her instead of posing for the camera. In order to capture her attention, the photographer began flashing bright colors behind the camera. The plan worked and he was able to take his pictures.

When he told Erin that he was finished, she refused to get off her seat and kept looking in the direction where she had just seen all of the flashing lights. Then Erin turned to her parents and signed her own version of *all gone*, moving her hands from the center outward. This was her way of asking if the light show was over.

Keith and Deirdre were happy to understand what was on Erin's mind—and to see that she was eager to communicate.

CHAPTER FIVE
Advanced Baby Signs

WHEN WILL MY BABY BE READY TO SIGN PHRASES?

As your baby's signing vocabulary expands, he or she will be ready to take signing to the next level—combining two or more signs into short phrases. Now your baby will be able to communicate complex ideas with you! Your baby will probably start by combining *more* with another sign. For example, you may begin to see the signs for *more juice*, *more cookie*, or even *more book*.

❚❚ Parents who enter into a dialogue with their children . . . are more likely to have children whose intellectual and ethical development proceeds rapidly and surely. *❚❚*

Mary Field Belenky, Blythe Mcvicker Clinchy, Nancy Rule Goldberger, and Jill Mattuck Tarule, Women's Ways of Knowing

WHAT ARE SOME TYPICAL WORD COMBINATIONS?

You will be amazed at how quickly your child will begin to combine signs. Here are some signs that are easily combined and likely to be of interest to your child:

More is a great sign to combine with other signs because this word helps your baby to ask for more of what he or she wants. Some examples are: *more + drink, more + eat.*

Where helps your child ask for unseen objects. Some examples are: *where + cookie, where + dog.*

All gone helps your baby mark the end of activities or comment on something that is no longer in sight. This sign also helps you to transition your baby from one activity to another. Some examples are: *all gone + milk, all gone + balloon.*

Mommy and *baby* are favorite signs to combine with animal words, such as *mommy duck* and *baby duck*.

Big and *little* are also useful signs. They can be used to describe almost anything, such as *big dog* and *little baby*.

Even after your child begins to talk, he or she will combine spoken words with signs. You may notice that your child says a word and combines it with a sign he cannot yet say. There will come a point when you won't be able to differentiate between what words your baby can say or sign!

Big   Train

WHEN WILL MY BABY BE READY TO SWITCH FROM SIGNING TO TALKING?

Eventually, your baby will recognize many signed words and will be able to use them in the correct context. The next step is talking! As your child begins to speak, he or she will pair words with familiar signs. Your child also may combine spoken words with words he or she is not yet able to verbally express.

For example, the word *flower* is more difficult for a toddler to pronounce than *mine*. So your child may sign *flower* and say *mine* to tell you that the flower belongs to him or her.

Chances are, as your child begins to speak more words, he or she will start to neglect signs in favor of words. Still, there will probably be times when he or she may also sign for clarification or emphasis.

Flower

Every baby is unique—the rate at which children begin combining signs and speaking will differ from one to the next!

WHAT SHOULD I DO IF I WANT MY CHILD TO LEARN SIGNING AS A SECOND LANGUAGE?

Many parents wonder if their children will continue to rely on signing once they've begun to speak. Most likely your child will drop the signs you once used together and will begin to rely solely on verbal communication.

If you decide that you want your child to continue signing as a second language (so that he or she is able to communicate with deaf and hard-of-hearing peers), you should continue to sign together. Continue introducing new signs and practicing older, learned signs so that they are not forgotten.

Many hearing families continue to use baby sign language as their children become older. It is a wonderful way to exchange private messages (such as "I love you" or "I'm afraid") when in the presence of others.

" To have another language is to possess a second soul. *"*

Charlemagne

Love

WHAT IF MY CHILD IS BILINGUAL?

Speaking two languages is like any other skill. To do it well, children need lots of practice, which parents and caregivers can help provide. Many bilingual families wonder if and how baby sign language will fit into the picture when their baby is already hearing two languages (such as English and Spanish). Because signs reduce your baby's confusion by providing a consistent symbol for objects, the idea of signing in a bilingual home makes perfect sense!

To teach your child two languages: Use two languages from the start. Give your child many opportunities to practice and hear both languages.

** As your baby progresses from one milestone to the next, remember that he doesn't really leave any of them behind. In order to grow and develop . . . he must continually build on and strengthen all of the steps that have gone before. **

Stanley I. Greenspan and Nancy Thorndike Greenspan, First Feelings: Milestones in the Emotional Development of Your Baby and Child

Most children have the capacity to learn two or more languages.

WHAT IF MY CHILD IS HAVING DIFFICULTIES WITH BABY SIGN LANGUAGE?

As you continue to sign with your baby, you may come upon problems that you don't know how to deal with. Keep these points in mind as you continue working on better communication with your child:

- Be consistent when choosing words. Use words that are in your child's day-to-day vocabulary, such as *milk*, *more*, or *cookie*.

- Start with a handful of signs and use them often. Children who see a lot of signing will get the hang of it quickly.

- Don't take on too much at once! Some parents are tempted to sign every word when they realize how much fun baby sign language can be. Using just a few signs consistently will be more effective for both you and your baby.

- Encourage your child to sign to communicate his needs. For example, if you know that your baby is ready for a bottle of milk and has begun to whine, rather than giving into the whining, sign *milk* so that he or she can realize there is another way to ask for things.

- Use signs that are motivating for your child. Your child will want to sign if he or she knows that gestures will be rewarded with favorite toys or snacks.

BROTHER-SISTER SIGNING

Ever since his parents started teaching his younger sister how to sign, two-year-old Noah thinks he is a baby sign language expert! During snack time one afternoon, his mother Debbie allowed Noah to share his Cheerios with Talia, his seven-month-old sister. After a short while, Debbie noticed that Noah was signing *eat* to Talia by placing his fingertips to his lips. As Debbie was about to praise Noah for sharing with his little sister, she saw that her daughter was signing *more* back to Noah by tapping her fingertips together.

Although Talia had demonstrated the sign for *more* on previous occasions, Debbie was thrilled that her children were communicating to each other using sign language. For many months Debbie had been telling Noah that one day, with his encouragement, Talia would sign back to him—and now it was finally happening.

CHAPTER SIX

Fun with Baby Sign Language

RHYMES, SONGS, AND GAMES

Children love rhymes, songs, and games, especially when they are accompanied by finger play and gestures. Introducing baby signs during playtime is motivating and fun for your child. It is also a great opportunity to teach the signs. Songs and rhyme have repeated patterns and sequences of words and rhythm. Included in this chapter are some rhymes, songs, and games that you can share with your baby. The italicized words indicate the appropriate baby sign to use.

And remember—you can take any song your child enjoys and include a baby sign in it!

THE EENSY WEENSY SPIDER

The eensy weensy spider (*spider* going up*)
Went up the water spout.
Down came the rain (*rain*)
And washed the spider out. (*all gone*)
Out came the sun (*sun*)
And dried up all the rain. (*rain*)
And the eensy weensy spider (*spider* going up)
Went up the spout again.

* Touch pointer on one hand to thumb on the other. Then touch pointer on the other hand to the other thumb. Continue alternating in a continuous motion upword.

Spider   Rain   Sun   All Gone

OLD MCDONALD

Old McDonald had a farm,
E-I-E-I-O
And on that farm he had a cow, (*cow*)
E-I-E-I-O
With a MOO MOO here and a MOO MOO there
Here a MOO
There a MOO
Everywhere a MOO MOO
Old McDonald had a farm,
E-I-E-I-O!
(Repeat using *horse*, *chicken*, *bird*, *pig*)

Cow   Horse   Bird   Pig

TWINKLE, TWINKLE, LITTLE STAR

Twinkle, twinkle, little star, (*stars*)
How I wonder what you are.
Up above the moon (*moon*) so high,
Like a diamond in the sky.
Twinkle, twinkle, little star, (*stars*)
How I wonder what you are.

Stars   Moon

THE WHEELS ON THE BUS

The wheels on the bus (*car*) go round and round
Round and round
Round and round.
The wheels on the bus (*car*) go round and round
All through the town.

Car

Baby

The babies (*baby*) on the bus say, "Peekaboo,
Peekaboo, peekaboo."
The babies (*baby*) on the bus say, "Peekaboo,"
All through the town.

Mommy

The mommies (*mommy*) on the bus say, "I love you, (*love*)
I love you, I love you."
The mommies (*mommy*) on the bus say, "I love you,"
(*love*)
All through the town.

Love

ROW YOUR BOAT

Row, row, row your boat (*boat*)
Gently (*gentle*) down the stream,
Merrily merrily, merrily, merrily,
Life is but a dream.

Boat   Gentle

FIVE LITTLE MONKEYS

Five little monkeys (*monkey*)
Jumping on the bed,
One fell off and bumped his head.
Mommy called (*mommy*, *telephone*) the doctor
And the doctor said,
"NO MORE MONKEYS (*monkey*)
JUMPING ON THE BED!"
Repeat using:
Four little monkeys . . .
Three little monkeys . . .
Two little monkeys . . .
One little monkey . . .

Monkey

Telephone

Mommy

BENJAMIN SIGNS AT SCHOOL

At two years old, Benjamin has been using sign language for over a year. For Benjamin, signs are everywhere, including in his favorite songs. Because Karine, his mother, signs to him as often as possible, Benjamin has learned to incorporate signs, even when he is away from his parents. While in school, many of the songs Benjamin's teachers have taught to the class include the use of gestures. This, of course, has added to the fun of learning.

One afternoon during music class, the children were learning a new song about butterflies and flowers. Benjamin had never heard the song before but began to sign. Every time his teacher sang a familiar word, Benjamin made a sign for it. Eventually, his teacher caught on to what he was doing and slowed down the song so that all the children could make signs for the words. Here Benjamin is signing *butterfly* by linking his thumbs and wiggling his fingers.

HERE'S A SPECIAL PLACE TO WRITE ABOUT YOUR CHILD'S PROGRESS AS HE/SHE LEARNS TO SIGN!

First sign: _____

Age when signed:_____

First phrase signed: _____

Age when signed: _____

First sentence signed: _____

Age when signed: _____

Favorite signs: _____

Made-up signs: _____

ADDITIONAL NOTES/STORIES

_____

_____

_____

_____

_____

_____

_____

_____

_____

_____

_____

ADDITIONAL NOTES/STORIES

_____

_____

_____

_____

_____

_____

_____

_____

_____

_____

_____

_____

ADDITIONAL NOTES/STORIES

_____

_____

_____

_____

_____

_____

_____

_____

_____

_____

_____

DICTIONARY OF BABY SIGNS

This section lists in alphabetical order all the signs included in this book and in the cards. These signs will give you and your little one a head start to many productive days of signing. As you become more proficient with signing, you'll find you need to refer to the signs less and less. However, continue to refer to them for inspiration or as a quick review. Remember to keep creating made-up signs as well.

Afraid
Protect body with palms open while cringing.

Airplane
With index and little finger up, swoop hand upward.

All Gone
Swoop hands from the center outward.

Angry
Open and close clawed hand while scowling.

Baby
Make rock-a-bye motion.

Babysitter
Link two index fingers together and bring them close to chest.

Ball
Trace a ball shape with hands.

Banana
*Make a peeling motion
down the index finger.*

Bath
*Make fists and rub up
and down chest.*

Big
*Keeping both index fingers and
thumbs up, move hands apart.*

Bird
*Hold index finger and thumb
close to mouth and open
and close like a bird's beak.*

Blanket
*Grasp and pull up an
imaginary blanket with
downturned hands.*

Boat
*Cup both hands and move them up
and down in a forward motion.*

Book
*Hold hands together and
open and close palms.*

Car
*Make a steering motion
with fists.*

Cat
*Trace whiskers on
cheek with fingers.*

Cereal
*Form an "O" with thumb
and index finger.*

Cold
*Hold arms close to
body and shiver.*

Cookie
*Twist fingertips in palm,
like a cookie cutter.*

Cow
*Make a "horn" with
little finger.*

Daddy
*Tap thumb on forehead
with fingers spread.*

Diaper
Pat hip.

Dirty
*Wiggle fingers of right
hand under chin.*

Dog
*Brush the back of one ear
a couple of times.*

Drink
Tip an imaginary glass to open lips, as if drinking.

Eat
Place fingertips to the lips.

Flower
Touch each side of nose with fingers.

Gentle
Stroke the back of the opposite hand.

Go
With both index fingers extended, point in the direction you are going.

Hair
Rub hair between fingers.

Happy
With flat hand, pat chest with an upward stroking movement.

Help
With fist on palm, move palm upward.

Hi/Bye
Hold hand in front of shoulder and wave fingers up and down.

Horse
Move fingers up and down in a motion similar to the flapping of a horse's ears.

Hot
With palm out, move hand up and down.

Hurt
Touch index fingers together.

Juice
Place one fist on top of the other fist and twist.

Light
Open and close fists.

Little
Face palms together and close.

Love
Cross fists over chest.

Milk
Open and close fists as if milking a cow.

Mommy
Tap thumb on cheek with fingers spread.

Monkey
Scratch under arms.

Moon
Raise palm and make circles.

More
Tap fingertips together.

Music/Song
Move hand back and forth rhythmically.

No
Close first two fingers on thumb.

Out/Outside
Pull one hand out of the other hand.

Pacifier
Suck on thumb and index finger.

Pig
Press finger into nose.

Play
With thumb and little finger up, twist both hands.

Please
Place hand over heart and move it in circles.

Quiet
Place index finger across lips.

Rain
Wiggle fingers while moving downwards.

Sad
Trace imaginary tears down cheek.

Share
Brush the little finger of one hand back and forth along the index finger of other hand as if dividing something.

Shoe
With thumbs facing inward, hit fists together twice.

Sleep
Rest head on hands and tilt head to the side.

Sorry
Make a circle on chest with fist.

Spider
Cross hands and wiggle fingers while moving them forward.

Stars
Raise hands and wiggle fingers.

Stop
Use side of hand to hit palm sharply.

Sun
Curve both hands over head.

Telephone
Hold pinky finger and thumb out and place next to ear.

Thank You/You're Welcome
Pull the fingertips of one hand away from chin.

Toothbrush
Move finger across teeth.

Train
Move fist up and down as if pulling a whistle.

Wait
With upturned hands, wiggle fingers with the left hand forward.

Want
Hold palms facing upward and form claws with fingers, pulling them towards body.

Water
Use extended index, middle, and ring fingers to form a "W." Tap the "W" on the chin twice.

Where
Point index finger up and move back and forth from side to side.

Yes
Make a fist and move it up and down at the wrist while nodding head.

INDEX

Acredolo, Linda, 12, 13, 116

Alaska, University of, 13

American Sign Language (ASL), 8, 10, 11, 14, 70

Bilingual, 82

California, Davis; University of, 13

Dancing with Words: Signing for Hearing Children's Literacy, 20

Daniels, Marilyn, 201

Daycare, 68–69

"Eensy Weensy Spider, The," 62, 90

"Five Little Monkeys," 95

Frustration, 7, 18

Garcia, Joseph, 13

Goodwyn, Susan, 12, 13

Made-up signs (home signs), 70-71, 72

National Institute of Child Health and Human Development, 13

"Old MacDonald," 91

Research, 14, 20, 29

"Row Your Boat," 94

Signs

Afraid, 54, 104

Airplane, 60, 104

All Gone, 24, 51, 76, 90, 104

Angry, 54, 104

Baby, 23, 59, 77, 93, 104

Babysitter, 104

Ball, 16, 58, 105

Banana, 50, 69, 105

Bath, 52, 105

Big, 59, 77, 105

Bird, 61, 91, 105

Blanket, 52, 105

Boat, 94, 106

Book, 19, 27, 52, 75, 106

Butterfly, 97

Car, 60, 93, 106

Cat, 27, 47, 106

Cereal, 23, 34, 35, 51, 106

Cold, 57, 106

Cookie, 50, 75, 76, 84, 107

Cow, 91, 107

Daddy, 107

Diaper, 59, 107

Dirty, 57, 107

Dog, 27, 61, 76, 77, 107

Drink, 27, 51, 76, 108

Eat, 27, 34, 51, 65, 76, 87, 108

Flower, 27, 61, 78, 108

Gentle, 57, 94, 108

Go, 108

Hair, 59, 108

Happy, 54, 109

Help, 56, 109

Hi/Bye, 31, 53, 109

Horse, 8, 91, 109

Hot, 56, 109

Hurt, 21, 57, 109

Juice, 17, 50, 75, 110

Light, 53, 110

Little, 59, 77, 110

Love, 55, 81, 93, 110

Milk, 24, 27, 44, 45, 50, 84, 85, 110

Mommy, 77, 93, 95, 110

Monkey, 39, 95, 111

Moon, 53, 92, 111

More, 24, 27, 44, 51, 75, 76, 84, 87, 111

Music/Song, 20, 58, 111

No, 57, 111

Out/Outside, 61, 111

Pacifier, 52, 112

Pig, 39, 91, 112

Play, 59, 112

Please, 55, 112

Quiet, 53, 112

Rain, 60, 90, 112

Sad, 54, 113

Share, 55, 113

Shoe, 58, 113

Sleep, 15, 53, 113

Sorry, 55, 113

Spider, 62, 90, 113

Stars, 61, 92, 114

Stop, 56, 114

Sun, 60, 90, 114

Telephone, 58, 95, 114

Thank You/You're Welcome, 55, 114

Toothbrush, 53, 69, 114

Train, 61, 77, 115

Wait, 56, 115

Want, 55, 115

Water, 51, 63, 115

Where, 76, 115

Yes, 57, 115

"Twinkle, Twinkle, Little Star," 92

"Wheels on the Bus, The," 93

ABOUT THE AUTHOR

Karine Shemel Rosenberg is a speech language pathologist at the Albert Einstein College of Medicine and at the Children's Hospital at Montefiore Medical Center. She works with children who have been diagnosed with a variety of impairments, including speech and language delays, craniofacial anomalies, genetic disorders, and hearing-impairments, many of whom are candidates for cochlear implantation.

Rosenberg studied baby sign language for several years before she began using it with her son when he was an infant. She currently lives in New York City with her husband and two-year-old son, Benjamin.